Much of our planet is covered by sea. The sea is home to thousands of aquatic animals. Where an animal lives is called its habitat.

Many of the animals that live under the sea are fish. Fish breathe with their gills. The gills are on the sides of the fish's body.

scales

gills

A fish's body is covered with scales.

Not all of the animals that live under the sea are fish. Some are mammals. Mammals have to come up to the surface of the sea to breathe air.

dolphin

blowhole

A dolphin is a mammal. It has a hole on its head called a blowhole, which it uses to take in air. When it dives under the sea it closes its blowhole.

The whale shark is the biggest fish on our planet, but is it a whale, or is it a shark? It is in fact a sort of shark. A whale shark's mouth is so large that a person could fit inside it. But this huge fish would not eat a person. Whale sharks only eat plankton. Plankton is made up of thousands of very small animals, eggs and little bits of seaweed.

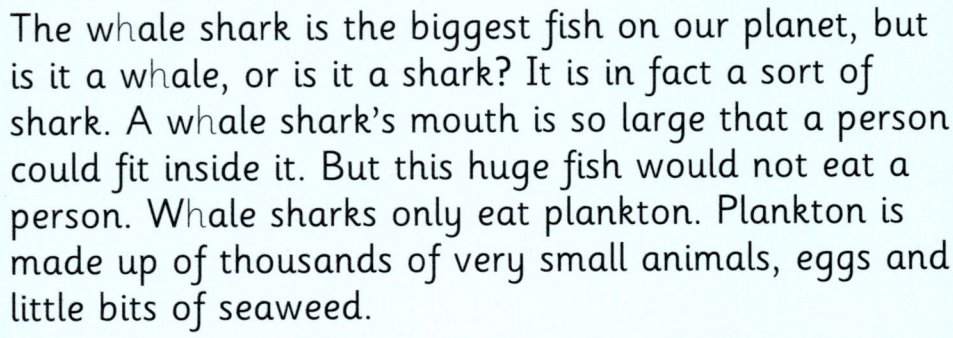

whale shark

mouth

On average, whale sharks grow to be about 10m long. This is about the same length as six adults lying in a line.

gills

As a whale shark swims, it opens its mouth and the sea flows in and then out again over its gills. The floating plankton gets filtered out in the brush-like parts of the gills. Then the whale shark eats all of the bits of plankton that have been trapped.

There is a huge amount of plankton in the sea. Hundreds of incredibly small animals and leaf-like things float in every drop. Some of the animals that make up the plankton are only the size of a grain of salt!

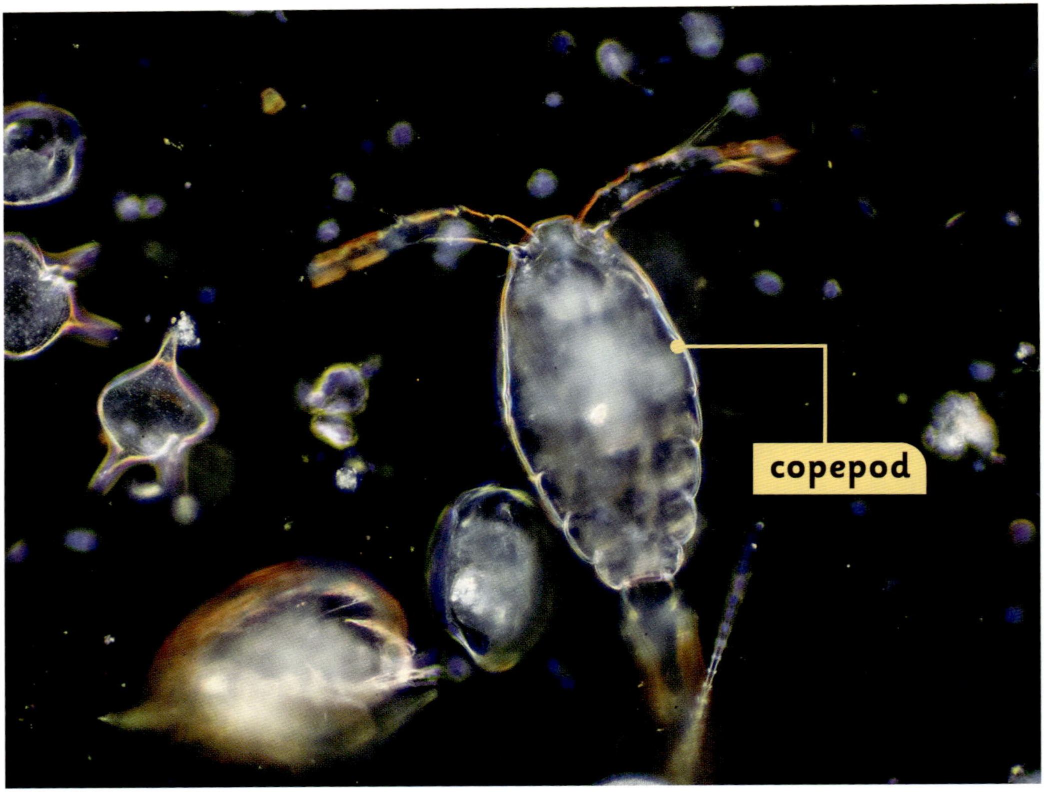

copepod

A number of the animals floating in the plankton, such as copepods and shrimps, will stay small for the whole of their lives. But others are the young of bigger animals, such as starfish, crabs and jellyfish.

young crab

newly hatched starfish

The organisms are far too small for us to see without the help of a microscope (/**mie**crəscoap/). Images like these are taken with a camera that is attached to a microscope. The images show the animals fifty times bigger than they are in real life.

Like dolphins, whales are mammals and have to swim to the surface to breathe air. Like whale sharks, humpback whales feed on plankton.

A humpback whale has a small hump on its back, long pectoral fins and a knobbly head. Male humpback whales make long calls that sound like singing.

humpback whale

long pectoral fin

knobbly head

small hump

Sometimes, humpback whales leap into the air and then splash back down into the sea. It is spectacular to see.

Blue whales are the biggest animals that have ever lived on our planet. An adult blue whale can be 30m long, and as heavy as twenty-five elephants!

blue whale

krill

Blue whales eat extremely small shrimp-like animals called krill. An adult blue whale can eat forty million krill each day!

In tropical seas, lots of animals live on coral reefs. A coral reef looks like it is made of rock, but in fact it is made from lots of little animals called coral polyps (/**po**lips/). Some coral polyps have a hard, rock-like skeleton.

hard skeleton

coral polyps

tentacles

Some coral polyps also eat plankton. They catch the plankton with their arm-like tentacles.

Millions of corals join together to make a colony. These join up to make a coral reef. Once a coral dies, its hard skeleton stays as part of the reef. Over a long time, the reef gets bigger and bigger.

fish that live on the reef

live coral

old coral skeletons

Coral reefs are sometimes called the 'rainforest of the sea' because so many different organisms live in or on them.

Sea anemones (/ənemənēz/) are animals that look like flowers. Some sea anemones live on coral reefs. A sea anemone has lots of tentacles around its mouth. The tentacles grab and sting small fish. Then the anemone sucks the fish into its mouth.

Clownfish live on coral reefs. When they see a bigger fish or a predator, clownfish hide in the tentacles of sea anemones.

A predator is an animal that hunts and eats other animals.

sea anemone

clownfish

stinging tentacles

The clownfish do not get stung by the sea anemones because a clownfish's body is covered with a layer of slime that stops the stings hurting the fish!

An eel is a fish that looks more like a snake. Eels have strong jaws, lots of sharp teeth and a long, thin body with fins. There are many different types of eel. A conger eel's body can be up to 3m long!

electric eel

This fish is called an electric eel, but it is not really an eel at all. It is a sort of knifefish. As its name suggests, this fish can give you an electric shock. It catches other fish by stunning them with an electric shock, and then sucks them into its mouth to eat.

Moray eels live in caves in the coral reefs. At night-time, the hungry eels get ready to hunt. They wait for another fish to swim by; then they burst out of their cave and attack!

Moray eel

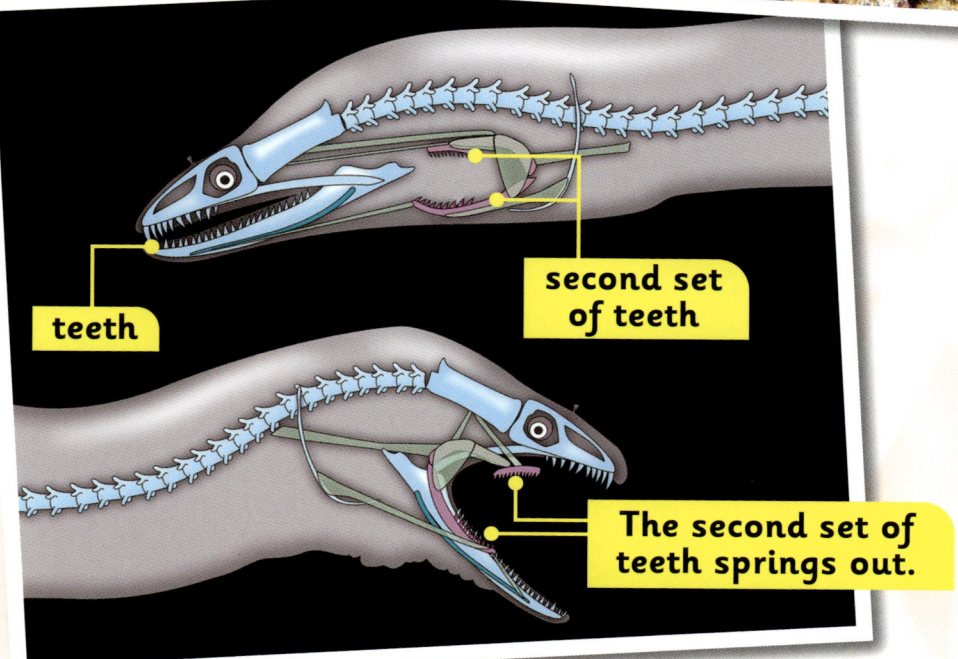

teeth

second set of teeth

The second set of teeth springs out.

The eel grabs the fish with its teeth so it cannot escape. Then something gruesome happens. Inside the eel's throat there is a second set of teeth. These teeth spring out and grab the fish to drag it further down the eel's throat!

A seahorse has a head like a horse, but it is really a fish! Seahorses pair up for life. Each morning, the seahorse pairs swim in the sea with their tails curled together.

seahorse

Seahorses live in the seaweed that grows on the sea bed.

When it is time to mate, seahorses put their abdomens together. Then the mother seahorse sprays hundreds of eggs into a bag-like pouch in the father's body. When the young seahorses have hatched, they pop out of their father's pouch and swim off.

father seahorse

young seahorse

pouch

A leafy seadragon is a seahorse with a clever disguise. It has green and yellow bits of skin on its body that look just like seaweed. As it swims along it looks like it is just a bit of floating seaweed, so its predators are fooled into not attacking it.

These are just some of the many interesting animals that live under the sea.

A seahorse has a hard skeleton on the outside of its body.